a taste of Italy

specials

Cooking with Anna

Fun and Healthy Italian and Mediterranean Recipes

Anna Carera

Contents

Foreword

This is my fifth cookbook and it offers a collection of Italian and Mediterranean dishes that I adapted to my taste. To make reading and learning about my recipes easier, I colored:

appetizers in green,

*first courses in **blue**,*

*second courses in **red**,*

*desserts in **brown**,*

*gluten free dishes in **purple**.*

I hope my readers will enjoy these simple recipes and will try to use a few of them in order to create a full Italian meal. On Sundays, on holidays, on special occasions, Italians love to eat a 4-course meal which consists in: an appetizer, a first course, a second course and a dessert.

Readers can choose among the several recipes and create different combinations of menus.

I also explain my own way of cooking and eating fun and healthy food and things to avoid in order to lose weight.

Weight shouldn't be an obsession but food needs to be homemade and healthy all the time!

A healthy Mediterranean diet

In this cookbook there are original recipes from the Mediterranean area.

The concept that Italian cooking is fattening is wrong: we eat rather small amount of food and never mix some ingredients. The quantities I give in each recipe are for 4 people.

I am not a dietician nor a nutritionist, so the following are just suggestions that I take into consideration since I cook every day and eat these dishes daily.

My personal experience is that you can also lose weight eating fun Italian food if you:

1   *Eat pasta 3 times a week, max. 90 grams with vegetable sauces;*

2   *Avoid cream and fattening sauces;*

3   *Never mix bread with pasta;*

4   *Eat homemade and not preserved food;*

5   *Eat a simple breakfast with homemade bread and jam or cereals, a lovely salad at lunch and an honest dinner with just one main course;*

6   *If you eat* pasta, *don't eat another course, eat vegetable and fruit;*

7   *Don't exaggerate with sugar or salt, use very little;*

8   *Replace salt with aromatic herbs and chili flakes;*

9   *Eat white meat, such as chicken or turkey, a couple of times a week;*

10   *Eat red meat once a week;*

11   *Eat lots of vegetables with extra virgin olive oil (evo), balsamic vinegar, very little salt and aromatic herbs.*

If you want to lose weight, remember to avoid:

1   *Bread, or just one slice of homemade bread without preservatives;*

2   *Wine, or just a small glass of red wine - that has great anti-oxidant properties;*

3   *Creams, mayo and any fattening dressing;*

4   *Desserts.*

Set up a nice table, put a slice of fresh lemon in your still mineral water and enjoy a lovely meal.

You can also lose weight and have a slice of homemade *pizza* once a week, just eat it with a fresh salad.

Just remember:

quantities and quality of ingredients make the difference

The ideal meal to lose weight

Why we eat *pasta* almost daily…

Pasta plays a fundamental role in the Mediterranean diet.

Homemade *pasta* is very healthy and, when you use excellent quality flours, you know exactly what you eat.

Pasta has several health benefits such as:

It provides folic acid;

It is cholesterol free;

It provides slow sugars which make us feel satisfied and full longer;

It allows you to use all sorts of food you like the most with your dish of pasta*;*

Whole grain pasta *also protects against stomach and colon cancers;*

It is proven by recent studies that people who eat pasta *as part of the Mediterranean diet lose more body fat than those who did not;*

It is low in sodium and food high in salt content might provoke heart diseases, high blood pressure and diabetes;

It is low in fat, it has about half a gram of fat per serving;

It helps keeping blood sugar regulated due to its low glycemic index, thus preventing diabetes and obesity;

Pasta *can also be gluten-free so those who are sensitive to gluten can enjoy a lovely dish of* pasta*;*

What is essential to keep a dish of *pasta* healthy is to cook a healthy sauce.

In my recipes, it is easy to note how light and healthy my sauces are.

I don't fry

I don't use cream

I recommend to eat small portions

I don't use much salt and recommend aromatic herbs instead

I have included many *pasta* recipes in this book because of all the above reasons and I highly encourage my readers to make fresh *pasta* at home.

It is cheaper, healthier and great fun and you can use the best and healthier flours!

Fresh pasta when it is dry

About my recipes

You can eat any of the dishes described in this cookbook regularly, this is definitely how I cook every day.

My recipes are simple and their explanation is simple. It is my intention to encourage anyone to experiment in the kitchen and provide fun and healthy meals to their families.

Explanations are easy to follow. Use a scale so you can click on ounces or grams and it is very easy. Otherwise at the end of this book, there is a conversion chart

Time of cooking could vary from oven to oven; the first time, always check your food while cooking.

What is called cream in this book is *panna da cucina* which literally means cooking cream and in many countries it does not exist, if you can't find it, use something similar.

I cook mostly northern Italian dishes because I live near Lake Garda, between Milan and Venice, and I also enjoy cooking adapted and revised Mediterranean recipes.

In northern Italy, the climate can range from cool to very cold in winter. Our dishes reflect the richness and climate of our area: *risotto* cooked with delicate broth, creamy *polenta* rich with butter, classic bean soup called *pasta e fagioli*, and all sorts of *pasta* dishes with light sauces.

Cooking tends to be lightly prepared and simple.

Because I am Italian and live in Italy, some expressions, ingredients or words might seem strange; no worries, get in touch with me and I will explain.

It is so important to be creative in the kitchen and, most of all, in life.

I am not a cook nor a chef; I am an Italian *mamma* who has great passion in cooking, in writing and definitely in living.

I am always at my readers' disposal if they need an explanation or an online cooking class.

My cookbooks reflect my personality and my way of living, I am a simple person who leads a simple life.

Keep everything simple and you will find happiness.

Today, I invite you to cook with me...

Dinner in the garden by the pond

How to use this recipe book

It consists of 43 recipes, some interesting stories and anecdotes, and a few useful tips.

Try several recipes, choose the ones you prefer and then put together an Italian evening meal with:

a starter, a main course – either a first course or a second course – and a dessert.

Open a bottle of a good Italian wine and celebrate.

Life is about celebrating the gift of being alive and sitting around a table with your family and friends is a sweet celebration.

Dinner in the living room

Prosciutto e melone

Ingredients:

1 orange Italian melon

150 gr. of *prosciutto di Parma*, very thin slices

Cut the melon in slices: an average Italian melon will be cut in 8 or 10 slices, remove seeds and skin. Display the slices of melon in a lovely plate and wrap each slice with a slice of *prosciutto di Parma* (Parma ham).

Alternatively, put the slices over the melon and create a décor with them, like a wave wrapping the melon. Finish with inserting cute wooden sticks for the guests to use to pick up each slice of *prosciutto e melone*.

Stendino *(charcuterie rack)*

Ingredients:

1 wooden rack	slices of different charcuteries,
tomatoes and various vegetables	olives, different types of cheese

If you can find such a *charcuterie* rack, it looks really pretty; otherwise you can build it inserting two wooden sticks into the board and making a double rack on top of them where you will display the ham slices. Over grape leaves, if possible, display all sorts of cheese, tomatoes, olives and fruit. On top of it, display different sorts of charcuterie like in a laundry rack.

Torta salata *(savory tart)*

Ingredients:

1 sheet of round puff pastry

2 large zucchini

1 clove of garlic

extra virgin olive oil (evo)

100 gr. diced *pancetta* or *guanciale*

100 gr. *gorgonzola* or any soft cheese

300 ml. milk

2 eggs

Fry the finely sliced zucchini with some evo and a clove of garlic. Apart, fry diced *pancetta* without any additional fat. In a silicon mold or non-sticky oven mold, lay the puff pastry sheet, add the mixture of zucchini and diced *pancetta*, add the cheese cut in small pieces all over the mix. In a separate bowl, beat the eggs and mix with milk, spread over the pastry. In the oven for 40 minutes at 200° C.

Aromatic herbs focaccia

Ingredients:

500 gr. of flour	10 cherry tomatoes + aromatic herbs
100 ml. water	1 sachet of dry yeast
270 ml. milk	1 tablespoon of salt and 1 of sugar

Make the dough as in bread, mix well and knead for at least 10 minutes. Let the dough rest for 2 hours. Knead again. Give it a rectangular shape using your hands and put it on the oven tray over parchment paper.

Decorate with all aromatic herbs from the garden: fresh oregano, basil, parsley, sage, rosemary and flatten the herbs into the dough. Add some salt and chili flakes. Let it rest 2 more hours and then in the oven for about 20 minutes at 200° C.

The above picture is of an uncooked focaccia, in order to better show the ingredients

Onions, white beans and tuna fish salad

Ingredients:

2 large white or red onions

200 gr. of tuna fish in a can

fresh basil

chili flakes and herbs

salt, pepper and extra virgin olive oil

2 cans of white beans

Chop the onions finely, add the white beans and the tuna fish removing all oil from the cans. Add some lovely evo, salt, pepper, chili and any aromatic herbs of your preference. Mix well, put into the fridge for at least 1 hour so all flavors get nicely together. Serve with fresh basil on top.

Smoked ham and cheese puff pastry roses

Ingredients:

1 square puff pastry sheet

100 gr of sliced smoked ham

100 gr. of *gorgonzola* or any soft cheese

or *mortadella* or Parma ham

On a flat square sheet of puff pastry, lay the thin slices of smoked ham, or *mortadella* or Parma ham, add the soft cheese of your taste over. To make it creamier, I previously dilute it with a spoon of milk.

Then roll it and cut it into slices. In a silicon mold, put each slice and open it as a rose with its petals. In the oven for 20 minutes at 200° C.

Italian katchapuri *for 3 people*

Ingredients:

500 gr. flour

2 eggs + 3 eggs on top

diced *pancetta* or smoked ham

100 ml. water and 100 ml. milk

1 sachet of dry yeast, some melted butter

5 gr. salt and 5 gr. sugar

200 gr. *provolone*

200 gr. *mozzarella*

Dilute the yeast in lukewarm water. In a bowl, beat the eggs with milk. Add the yeast and mix well, then add the regular flour, salt, sugar and knead. Let it rest for 2 hours. Apart mix the cheeses with the eggs. On a board, roll the dough in 3 parts, give a boat shape rolling each side up and closing the two side edges, add the mix and the *pancetta* on each side. Brush all edges with melted butter. Cook at 200° C for ten minutes, then remove, make a hole in the center using a spoon and add 1 egg, cook again for extra 10 minutes.

Italian tartiflette

Ingredients:

5 potatoes	salt, pepper
1 clove of garlic	evo
150 gr. diced *pancetta*	chili flakes
100 gr. *Parmigiano* or Emmenthal	3 *mozzarella fiordilatte*

Cut the potatoes in small flat slices. In a non-sticky oven pan pour some evo, aromatic herbs and chili flakes with very little salt. Mix well. Add the *Parmigiano* or Emmenthal and cook at 190° degrees for 20 minutes, take them out of the oven, mix again and add the *mozzarella* slices and bacon on top and put it back into the oven for 20 extra minutes.

If you like onions, at the beginning add a couple of finely chopped onions.

You might also want to add half of a glass of white wine.

Sugo al pomodoro *(tomato sauce)*

Ingredients:

4 large organic Pachino or Roma
tomatoes

15 cherry tomatoes

evo

salt

pepper

oregano

aromatic herbs

250 gr. *polpa di pomodoro* Mutti

lemon thyme

In order to make a healthy and not heavy tomato sauce, I usually don't use the onions which require frying, I just pour evo, little salt, my aromatic herbs that I have finely chopped, chili flakes and all the tomatoes chopped using a knife. I add *polpa di pomodoro* Mutti because it adds a velvety consistency and I love the contrast between the pieces of tomatoes and the Mutti pulp. I cook covered for 15-20 minutes and then I uncover for 5 minutes to reduce the excess of liquid. Sprinkle with fresh lemon thyme.

Pici *with tomato sauce*

Ingredients:

400 gr. *pici* or homemade *spaghetti*   basil

salt, pepper   chili

evo   rosemary finely chopped,

1 clove of fresh garlic   the above mentioned tomato sauce

Boil *pici* or spaghetti in salted water.

Once *pici* are cooked and strained, pour them into the tomato sauce described in the previous recipe and cook for a couple of extra minutes. Serve adding freshly grated *Parmigiano* or *Grana Padano*, black pepper and fresh basil.

Braised tomatoes for tomato sauce

Ingredients:

20 cherry tomatoes

Cut each cherry tomato in a half.

Use a non-sticky pan.

Put the cherry tomatoes with their flat part over the pan and braise them for 10 minutes.

Turn them over and the open parts should show they are ready.

Add to any tomato sauce to add texture and an extra flavor.

Tagliatelle *with tomato sauce and lemon thyme*

Ingredients:

300 gr. fresh *tagliatelle*	olives
250 gr. tomato sauce, salt, pepper, evo	lemon thyme
20 cherry tomatoes	*Grana Padano* or *Parmigiano*

Boil fresh *tagliatelle* in salted water. Once they are cooked and strained, pour them into the tomato sauce described in the previous recipe and cook for a couple of extra minutes. Apart braise the cherry tomatoes cut in half and add a few of them on top of each plate, add some olives and small leaves of lemon thyme. Serve adding freshly grated *Parmigiano* or *Grana Padano* and black pepper.

Spaghetti aglio, olio e peperoncino

Ingredients:

400 gr. *spaghetti*	evo
4 cloves of garlic	*Grana Padano*
4 whole chili	

Boil *spaghetti* in salted water, once they are ready, strain them.

Apart chop garlic, chili finely chopped and make a sauce with evo in a saucepan. In order to make the sauce creamy, add one or two ladles of cooking water. The starch contained in cooking water makes it a lovely emulsion.

Pour the cooked *spaghetti* into the sauce and stir for a minute. Serve with grated *Grana Padano* cheese and add some fresh parsley.

Spaghetti all'Amatriciana

Ingredients:

400 gr. *spaghetti*

120 gr. *Pecorino* cheese

ground peppercorns

200 gr. *guanciale* (pork cheeks)

200 gr. *San Marzano pelati* (peeled tomatoes)

Boil the *spaghetti* in salted water. Apart cook diced *guanciale*, which is pork cheeks or *pancetta*. Prepare a small tomato sauce with *pelati* (peeled tomatoes), add the *guanciale* and the cooked and strained *spaghetti*. Serve with freshly ground peppercorns and *Pecorino* cheese. Personally, I don't use too much tomato sauce in order to better appreciate *guanciale* and *Pecorino* cheese.

The story of spaghetti all'Amatriciana

This dish was mentioned for the first time in 1816 when it was served at the court of the Pope. In the 19th century, near Piazza Navona in Rome, there was an alley called de Matriciani, then named Amatriciani, and a square where the Grici (or Sabini, people from the Sabinia area) held a market, sold bread, salame and cheese from the Sibillini mountains. This sauce comes from *gricia* or *griscia*, a dish of *spaghetti* or *maccheroni* flavored with evo, pepper and *guanciale* (pork cheeks) from the small town of Grisciano. The addition of the tomato sauce goes even back to 1600.

The first written mention of this Amatriciana dish is to be found in the cookbook of the Roman cook Francesco Leonardi who served it at the Pope court. It was a banquet in honor of Francis I Emperor of Austria organized by Pope Pius VII in April 1816. Leonardi worked for the French court and Richelieu, in Poland, England and Turkey as well as as chef for Catherine II of Russia. In 1790, he wrote a 7 volume cooking encyclopedia named *L'Apicio Moderno* describing all sorts of food preparations.

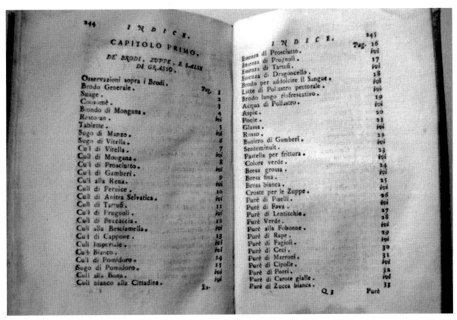

Spaghetti *with 2 color tomatoes and black garlic*

Ingredients:

400 gr. *spaghetti*

grated organic lemon

black garlic

a few leaves of basil

250 gr. red and yellow cherry tomatoes

salt, pepper and evo

chili and rosemary finely chopped

100 gr. *Parmigiano* or *Grana Padano*

A couple of hours before serving this dish, wash and cut in half the yellow and red cherry tomatoes. Add evo, salt, black garlic, black pepper and fresh basil. Cover and let it marinate. Boil *spaghetti* in salted water. Once cooked and strained, pour them into the tomato sauce and serve with fresh tomatoes. Especially in summer *spaghetti* and fresh tomatoes are particularly delicious. Serve adding freshly grated *Parmigiano* or *Grana Padano*, black pepper and fresh basil.

Spaghetti *with mussels*

Ingredients:

400 gr. *spaghetti*	500 gr. mussels
homemade tomato sauce	chili flakes
evo	fresh parsley
salt and pepper	

Cook the mussels in the tomato sauce whose recipe has been previously described.

Boil *spaghetti* in salted water, once cooked and strained, add them for a few minutes to the tomato and mussels sauce.

Serve with fresh parsley and sprinkle with grated organic lemon, lemon is a fantastic and fresh addition to any tomato sauce.

Spaghetti al pesto

Ingredients:

400 gr. *spaghetti*   40 ml. of evo

100 gr. *Pecorino* cheese   40 gr. almonds

50 gr. basil leaves

In a grinder put the basil leaves, add *Pecorino* cheese, almonds, evo and make it very smooth, add a spoon of cooking water if needed.

Boil the *spaghetti* in salted water, once cooked, strain them. In a saucepan, cook the homemade pesto sauce with the cooked spaghetti for a couple of minutes.

Sprinkle your plate with more *Pecorino* cheese, add a leaf of basil and a couple of almonds as a decoration.

Scialatielli

Ingredients:

400 gr. durum wheat flour	1 egg
30 gr. *Pecorino* cheese	10 ml. of evo oil
3 basil leaves	50 gr. of butter

In a bowl, beat the egg with melted butter, chop the basil leaves, add oil, *Pecorino* cheese, milk and flour.

Stir well, knead and make a nice dough, cut with a pizza cutter in long stripes and then make shorter stripes.

They are very light and have a wonderful and delicate taste.

The story of scialatielli

Scialatielli is a particularly shaped kind of fresh *pasta* that is recognized in Italy as a traditional *pasta*.

They were created in 1976 by chef Enrico Cosentino, from the Amalfi Coast, after studying and researching for about 6 months. This handmade *pasta* shape and its recipe became famous in 1978 when the chef won the Entremetier Prize for this creation at the International Culinary Contest.

We are not sure about the meaning of the term, there are two possible translations:

1.   the first meaning considers the union of the terms "scialare", that is "to enjoy", and "tiella", which means "pan" that come together into *scialatielli*

2.   the second meaning focuses on "sciglià", that is "ruffled", because the *pasta* looks like ruffled hair when cooked

It is a fabulous type of *pasta* easy to make and enjoy all time of the year.

Scialatielli *with* olive taggiasche

Ingredients:

400 gr. homemade *scialatielli*

1 large zucchini

evo

salt and pepper

garlic

Grana Padano

fresh parsley,

chili and rosemary spices

olive taggiasche from Liguria

Make a lovely sauce cooking finely sliced zucchini in evo, salt, pepper, chili flakes, aromatic spices. Cook the *scialatielli* in salted water, when ready, strain them and pour them into the zucchini sauce. Serve with *Grana Padano* cheese and add some *olives taggiasche* from Liguria, small and very tasty olives.

Homemade pasta bows

Squares of pasta pinched in the middle

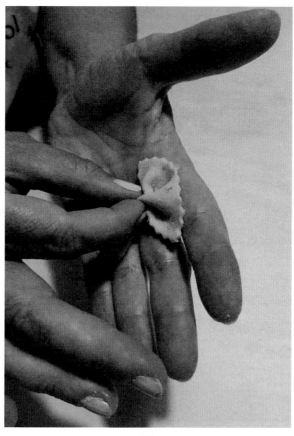

Homemade pasta *bows with tomatoes and olives*

Ingredients:

400 gr. of *pasta* bows	salt and pepper
200 gr. red and yellow cherry tomatoes	evo
chili flakes	100 gr. *olive taggiasche*
aromatic herbs	100 gr. *Parmigiano* or *Pecorino* cheese

Make a nice and smooth sauce cooking the cherry tomatoes cut in half, add evo, salt, pepper, chili flakes, aromatic spices. Cook *pasta* bows in salted water, when ready, strain them, and pour them into the tomato sauce. Braise some cherry tomatoes cut in half in a non-sticky pan. Serve adding on top of *pasta* bows: braised cherry tomatoes, some *olive taggiasche* from Liguria, small and very tasty olives, and grate *Parmigiano* o *Pecorino* chesee.

Fettuccine Alfredo

Ingredients:

400 gr. fettuccine

freshly ground peppercorns

a large ladle of cooking water

80 gr. butter

100 gr. *Parmigiano* or *Grana Padano*

Boil *fettuccine* in salted water, once ready, strain them. In a saucepan, amalgamate the *fettuccine* with 80 gr. of butter, one large ladle of cooking water and half of the cheese. Stir well. While stirring, the starch contained in the cooking water creates a creamy emulsion with butter and cheese.

Serve with a generous amount of *Parmigiano* or *Grana Padano* cheese and freshly ground peppercorns.

The real story of fettuccine *Alfredo*

In 1914 Alfredo, the owner of a restaurant in *Via della scrofa* in Rome, invented this recipe when he was trying to create something to give more energy to his wife who had just had a baby. She loved that simple dish so much that she suggested to include it in the restaurant menu. Quickly, it became the best specialty at that restaurant.

One day, the Hollywood actors Douglas Fairbanks and Mary Pickford tried that dish while they were having their honeymoon in Rome. They absolutely adored these *fettuccine*, so light and creamy and Douglas Fairbanks offered Alfredo two golden pieces of cutlery: a spoon and a fork where these special words were engraved:

To Alfredo: the King of Noodles

Alfredo's restaurant became the favorite restaurant among Hollywood stars and the recipe was brought to America but very much changed to favor American taste.

In 1942, Alfredo di Lelio sold this restaurant and in 1950 he opened "Il Vero Alfredo" in *Via Augusto Imperatore*, 30 in Rome where they still serve fettuccine Alfredo.

Secret:

The creamy texture is not given by any sort of cream. The emulsion is created by stirring the cooking water with butter. I also add a little amount of cheese. It is the starch which makes this nice and creamy emulsion, not any cream.

Homemade gluten free *spaghetti*

Ingredients:

100 gr. rice flour

100 gr. chickpeas flour

1 egg

80 gr. boiled potatoes

100 gr. *Grana Padano* or *Parmigiano*

10 ml. water

10 ml. milk

a splash of evo

In order to make homemade gluten free *spaghetti*, boil the potato, peel it and crush it using a fork. In a bowl, mix the two types of flours, add the potato, pour milk, water and oil. Mix well and knead. Make some small pieces and roll each one making some long *spaghetti*, 25 cm long. Cook in salted water and serve with tomato sauce and freshly grated *Parmigiano* or *Grana Padano* cheese.

Risotto *with tomatoes and* mozzarella

Ingredients:

400 gr. *vialone nano* o *carnaroli* rice

100 gr. butter and 2 tablespoons of evo

half of a shallot and a small carrot

sea salt, fresh parsley

1 liter of vegetable both

100 gr. *Parmigiano*

1 *stracciatella* o *buffalo mozzarella*

1 small glass of Port wine or white wine

200 gr *polpa di pomodoro* Mutti or a

homemade tomato sauce

Bring broth to boil and simmer for 20 minutes. Sauté half of a shallot and a small carrot with sea salt, butter and oil.

Add the tomato sauce and cook for 10 minutes. Pour the rice, toast it until it becomes translucent, it takes 2 minutes. Pour the Port wine or white wine. Let it evaporate. Add some broth when needed and cook approximately 13 minutes. It the end, add some *Parmigiano* cheese and extra butter to make it creamier. Decorate with fresh *stracciatella* or *buffalo mozzarella* on top of each plate.

Saffron risotto

Ingredients:

400 gr. *vialone nano* o *carnaroli rice*

100 gr. butter

2 tablespoons of evo

half of a shallot and a small carrot

sea salt

1 liter of vegetable both

0,20 gr. saffron

100 gr. *Grana Padano*

Bring broth to boil and simmer for 20 minutes. Sauté half of a shallot and a small carrot with sea salt, butter and oil.

Add the saffron previously diluted in a spoon of lukewarm water and cook for 10 minutes. Pour the rice, toast it until it becomes translucent. It takes 2 minutes. Pour the Port wine or white wine. Let it evaporate. Add some broth when needed and cook approximately 13 minutes. In the end, add some *Grana Padano* cheese and extra butter to make it creamier. Decorate with a few strings of saffron on top and more cheese.

Canederli (Knödel)

Ingredients:

250 gr. grated bread	2 eggs, 100 gr. *Grana Padano*
250 ml. milk	salt and pepper
150 gr. diced *pancetta* or smoked ham (*speck*)	chopped parsley
30 gr. regular flour	1 liter of vegetable broth
40 gr. butter	80 gr. butter
40 gr. finely chopped onion	8 sage leaves

Melt the butter with the onion. Dice the *speck* (smoked ham) or *pancetta* or bacon. In a bowl, mix milk with eggs, add salt and pepper and the finely chopped parsley. Add the bread, the diced smoked ham or *pancetta*, add the melted butter and stir well. Let this rest for 15 minutes.

Make balls of *Knödel* and let them rest on a parchment paper for further 20 minutes. You can also refrigerate covered and cook later. Boil in a vegetable broth for 15 minutes. Serve with broth or strain them and serve with a lovely sauce made with butter and sage. Add a generous amount of *Grana Padano* cheese. A typical dish from Northern Italy, not far from my area.

Spiedini *with red* radicchio *and asparagus*

Ingredients:

2 meat skewers per person (made with sausage, pork meat, beef meat, red and yellow peppers and onions)

500 gr. fresh asparagus

red *radicchio*

salt and pepper

evo

sesame seeds

BBQ the meat and vegetable skewers and pour just a sauce made with evo, salt and peppercorns. Apart, boil fresh asparagus, strain them and serve them with evo, salt and sesame seeds. Made again a sauce with evo, salt, peppercorns, balsamic glaze and pour over the red *radicchio* salad. Very simple, healthy and ideal in the summer.

Broccolo romanesco, mozzarella *and* tomatoes

Ingredients

1 *broccolo romanesco*

10 cherry tomatoes

salt and pepper

evo

250 gr. fresh *mozzarella*

aromatic herbs

In an oven pan, pour some evo and the *broccolo romanesco* cut in parts. Slice the fresh *mozzarella* and put it over the *broccolo*.

Add some cherry tomatoes and season with salt, pepper and aromatic herbs.

In the oven at 180° C for 30 minutes. Serve with any sort of meat.

Chicken thin slices with parsley

Ingredients:

8 thin slices of chicken	evo
parsley, salt and pepper	1 lemon
black garlic	a mixed salad

A very dietetic and healthy recipe: grill the thin slices of chicken in a non-sticky pan or plancha without adding any fat. Turn a few times.

Prepare a dressing with evo, salt, pepper, finely chopped fresh parsley, lemon juice and black garlic. Cover the meat with the dressing and turn it over in order to absorb the lovely flavors.

Serve with a fresh mixed salad and 1 slice of homemade sourdough bread with this fantastic sauce on top of it.

Fresh salad with octopus

Ingredients:

1 green salad	garlic
lemon slices	salt and pepper
oregano	evo
chili, olives	500 gr. of octopus

Boil the octopus in salted water: it needs to become tender, try it with a fork.

Prepare a lovely mixed salad with evo, aromatic herbs and lemon juice or balsamic vinegar

Mix it well and serve with octopus over it.

Add a slice of fresh lemon; or, if you prefer, instead of lemon, you can use a drizzle of balsamic vinegar and add some olives.

Piccata di vitello alla milanese

Ingredients:

8 slices of veal or chicken	capers
30 gr. butter	parsley
half of a glass of white wine	lemon
salt, pepper	regular flour

Flat the veal slices, flour each slice.

In a saucepan, melt the butter, add the floured slices of veal, cook well and pour the wine, let it evaporate.

Add the capers and serve with parsley and lemon slices.

Excellent with roasted potatoes cut in thin slices.

Saltimbocca *with sautéed Brussels sprouts*

Ingredients:

500 gr. of chicken or veal

10 slices of *Pecorino* cheese

10 leaves of sage

1 glass of white wine

10 slices of Parma ham or smoked ham

Take each slice of chicken or veal, lay one leaf of sage and one of *Pecorino* cheese, roll it and close with a couple of tooth sticks.

In a saucepan pour some evo, salt, pepper and cook the rolls for about 20 minutes. Pour the white wine, let it evaporate. Serve with polenta, potatoes or Brussels sprouts previously sautéed with evo, salt and pepper

Arista di maiale all'olio *(pork loin)*

Ingredients:

800 gr. of pork loin   salt and pepper

5 branches of rosemary   3 garlic cloves

10 sage leaves   1 glass of red wine

Open the pork loin as a book and do 4 cuts, 2 on each shorter side. Mix finely all aromas: 3 branches of rosemary, the sage leaves and the garlic. Insert this mix in the 4 cuts and all over the open pork loin. Close it and use a kitchen string to tight it on all sides. Use the 2 extra rosemary branches inserting them within the string, one on each side. Cook in a non-sticky pan with extra virgin olive oil, salt and pepper for 5 minutes, high flame until it gets a golden crust. Pour the red wine, let it evaporate. Cook again for 10 minutes on the stove. Take an oven pan, pour some evo and place the pork loin with its juice. Cook in the oven for 50 minutes at 160° C, check once in a while and turn the pork loin. It is perfect when it reaches the inside temperature of 68° C that you can check using the oven thermometer. Cut into slices and serve with its juice and polenta or roasted potatoes.

Chicken and 3 color peppers and tomatoes

Ingredients:

500 gr. chicken filets	evo
1 yellow, 1 green and 1 red pepper	salt and pepper
10 cherry tomatoes	aromatic herbs

Cook the chicken cut into small pieces with evo, salt, pepper and any favorite aromatic herbs for about 15 or 20 minutes.

Apart, cook in the oven the tomatoes and peppers with evo, salt and pepper for 30 minutes. Serve making layers of chicken, peppers and tomatoes, chicken, peppers and tomatoes ending with just a couple of pieces. Sprinkle with evo.

Veal spezzatino *with basmati rice*

Ingredients:

500 gr. veal for *spezzatino* (stew)	300 gr. basmati rice
200 gr. tomato sauce	chili flakes and aromatic herbs
1 onion	3 cloves, ½ liter of broth
evo	1 glass of red wine

Make a broth, I rather have a vegetable one because it is lighter. Apart fry one onion and pour the tomato sauce, the aromatic herbs and cloves chili flakes, little salt and after 5 minutes add the small veal pieces, stir and cook for 5 minutes. Add the wine and let it evaporate. Add the broth and cook for at least 2 hours, slowly, until meat is very tender.

Cook some basmati rice, I boil it in salted water and strain it. Serve the rice, add some of the *spezzatino* sauce and the veal on top of it. Alternatively, it is always excellent with roasted potatoes.

Ossobuco alla milanese

Ingredients:

2 *ossibuchi* per person	black peppercorns
50 ml. white wine	100 gr. tomato pulp
500 ml. meat broth	1 onion
50 ml. evo	50 gr. flour
50 gr. butter	

Make a good meat broth. Slice the onion and fry it slightly, pour the white wine and let it evaporate. Turn it off. In a bowl flour the *ossibuchi*, add salt and pepper and remove the excess of flour. In the saucepan where you fried the onions, remove them, add the butter and then the *ossibuchi*, medium high temperature for 4 minutes on one side, then turn on the other side for 4 minutes. At this point add the meat broth, the onions and the tomato sauce and cover. Cook for 35 minutes. Then turn gently the *ossibuchi* and cook again for 20 minutes.

Ingredients for *gremolada* sauce:

parsley	2 garlic cloves
1 organic lemon	

Apart prepare the *gremolada*: chop the garlic cloves, the fresh parsley and add some grated lemon zest. You can add the *gremolada* directly when serving the *ossibuchi* or serve the *gremolada* in a saucer and everyone will choose how to eat it.

They can be served with saffron *risotto*, *Parmigiano* cheese *risotto* or with roasted potatoes.

Ossobuco

Gremolada

Nonna *Doralice slow cooked beef*

Ingredients:

1 kg. beef shoulder

salt and pepper

1 cup of evo

½ cup white wine vinegar

4 cloves

3 bay leaves

1 finely chopped onion

Take a terracotta pot and pour a cup of extra virgin olive oil and ½ cup of white wine vinegar. Add salt, pepper, 4 cloves, 3 bay leaves, 1 finely chopped onion. Add the piece of beef shoulder, in Italian it is called *cappello di prete* and it becomes pulled beef. It becomes so tender that we don't even need to use a knife to cut it. Cover, open just a few times, slowly cook for 4 hours and then serve with roasted potatoes or *polenta*.

The white wine vinegar gives the dish a special fresh and unique twist and this recipe has been handed over 4 generations in my family and created by my great grandmother Doralice.

Beef carpaccio *wrap*

Ingredients:

500 gr. of extremely thin beef slices, as thin as Parma ham

100 gr. *Grana Padano*

evo

salt and pepper

green salad

capers

yellow tomatoes

mixed nuts

Pour the green salad on the plate and season it.

Lay the thin slices of raw beef over the salad, grate some *Grana Padano*, let it open in the middle where you will add tomatoes cut in small pieces and mixed nuts. Pour capers, evo, salt and pepper all over the plate. A beautiful and healthy Italian specialty with a different twist.

Gluten free chocolate cake

Ingredients:

3 eggs	100 ml. milk
150 gr. sugar	50 ml. evo
250 gr. rice flour	1 sachet of baking powder
50 gr. cocoa powder	half of a jar of strawberry jam

Beat the eggs, add the sugar and the baking powder. Add the cocoa powder, the rice flour, add milk and evo. Mix well.

Add a few spoons of strawberry jams on top of the mix. They will fall into the dough and they will create something like small craters.

Bake in the oven 40 minutes at 170° C.

Sprinkle with icing sugar.

Pineapple Pavlova

Ingredients:

6 egg whites	1 teaspoon white vinegar
300 gr. caster sugar and icing sugar for the finishing	1 pineapple and more fruit to decorate
	500 gr. whipped cream

Whisk the egg whites in a food processor or using a hand mixer (highest speed). Slowly add 300 gr. of caster sugar, a spoon at a time.

Keep going until the mixture is glossy and stiff. Whisk in a teaspoon of white vinegar.

Take two silicon molds or non-sticky containers, spread the meringue inside each container, creating a crater by making the sides a little higher than the middle. Bake at 80 °C. for two hours.

If necessary, after 1 hour put the meringue on the top below and the one below on the top for an even baking. Let the Pavlova cool completely inside the oven.

Once ready, take a plate, lay gently a meringue and cover it with whipped cream. Cut 150 gr. of pineapple and put them over the cream. Put the other meringue over the cream and pineapple mix.

Cover with whipped cream and add the top of the pineapple and other pieces of fruit as decorations such as grapes, an apricot, a peach or strawberries.

Sprinkle with icing sugar.

Tiramousse *cake*

Ingredients:

100 ml. milk

100 gr. chocolate

250 gr .yogurt

100 ml. milk to dip lady fingers biscuits

250 gr. cream

400 gr. lady fingers biscuits

150 gr. sugar

Mix yogurt, cream and sugar very well. Add chocolate and dilute with milk. In a bowl, add extra milk to dip lady fingers biscuits.

Take a glass container and make a layer of mousse, then add a layer of lady fingers dipped into milk, then another one of chocolate mousse. Sprinkle with icing sugar and/or cocoa powder. Refrigerate for 24 hours before serving.

English bread pudding

Ingredients:

12 slices of French flat bread	cashew nuts
50 gr. butter	sultanas
150 gr. sugar	300 ml. of milk
walnuts	3 eggs

In a round cake tin (7,1 inches), butter the tin, make one layer of bread slices previously buttered on both sides. On top of each slice add some nuts, walnuts and sultanas, then add another layer of bread slices buttered on both sides.

Whisk 3 egg whites, separately mix the egg yolks with sugar and then add the whisked whites. Incorporate 300 ml. of milk to the above mix and pour on top of the bread.

In the oven at 170° C. for about 30 minutes. Drizzle some caramel topping over each slice upon serving.

Apple tart

Ingredients:

1 kilo of apples lemon juice	150 gr. flour
150 gr. sugar	3 tablespoons of milk
2 eggs	1 table spoon of evo
1 sachet of baking powder	1 table spoon of Port or white wine

Slice 1 kg. of apples and pour lemon juice over.

In a bowl, add 150 gr. of sugar, 15 gr. of baking powder, two eggs and stir well.

Add the flour, grate some lemon zest on top, add 3 tablespoons of milk and 1 tablespoon of evo.

Add 1 tablespoon of Port wine and mix well. In the oven at 180° C for 45 minutes.

Crostata di arance *(orange tart)*

Ingredients:

250 gr. flour	a pinch of salt
1 egg	some lemon or vanilla extract
100 gr. butter	300 gr. of homemade orange marmalade
150 gr. sugar	

In a bowl, beat the egg with sugar. Add flour, melted butter and a pinch of salt. Mix it and knead it gently, make a ball and cover with cling film. Store in the fridge for 20 minutes. Take it out and, using the rolling pin, make a nice round pastry. Put the pastry in a non-sticky pan, cover with a lovely homemade orange jam or any other jam of your favorite taste and bake for 35 minutes at 180° C.

If you want to do the decoration, keep a small amount of pastry to make a net on top of it.

Apple strudel

Ingredients:

1 sheet of puff pastry   3 tablespoons of milk

4 apples   1 tablespoon of evo

150 gr. sugar   juice of 1 lemon

2 eggs

Slice the apples and pour the juice of 1 lemon, add the eggs beaten with sugar, milk and evo, bake in a non-sticky pan for 30 minutes. When ready, take an oven pan, lay the sheet of puff pastry, include the apple mix, if you like you may add sultanas. Seal the puff pastry sheet and bake in the oven at 200° C for 30 minutes.

Eat as it is or with other fruit or with *gelato,* Italian ice cream.

Conversion measurements chart: US vs European

Degrees

225 degrees F 104 degrees C

250 degrees F 120 degrees C

275 degrees F 135 degrees C

300 degrees F 149 degrees C

325 degrees F 163 degrees C

350 degrees F 177 degrees C

375 degrees F 191 degrees C

400 degrees F 204 degrees C

425 degrees F 218 degrees C

450 degrees F 232 degrees C

475 degrees F 246 degrees C

500 degrees F 260 degrees C

Common pan sizes

9 x 13 inch dish = 22 x 33 centimeter dish

8 x 8 inch dish = 20 x 20 centimeter dish

9 x 5 inch loaf pan = 23 x 12 centimeter loaf pan

9 inch cake pan = 22 centimeter cake pan

10 inch tart/cake pan = 25 centimeter tart/cake pan

Equivalents

1 stick of butter = 4 ounces, or 113 grams, or 1/2 cup

2 sticks of butter = 8 ounces, 230 grams, or 1 cup butter

1 ounce = 1/4 cup, or 40 grams (chocolate)

1 pound = 16 ounces, or 2 cups (dry)

Flour 1 cup flour = 140 grams

3/4 flour = 105 grams

1/2 cup flour = 70 grams

1/4 cup flour = 35 grams

Sugar (granulated)

1 cup sugar = 200 grams

3/4 cup sugar = 150 grams

2/3 cup sugar = 135 grams

1/2 cup sugar = 100 grams

1/3 cup sugar = 70 grams

1/4 cup sugar = 35 grams

Heavy cream

1 cup heavy cream = 235 grams

3/4 cup = 175g

1/2c = 90g

1/4c = 60g

US to Metric (Dry)

1 cup = 16 tbsp = 48 tsp = 240 ml

3/4 cup = 12 tbsp = 36 tsp = 180 ml

2/3 cup = 11 tbsp = 32 tsp = 160 ml

1/2 cup = 8 tbsp = 24 tsp = 120 ml

1/3 cup = 5 tbsp = 16 tsp = 80 ml

1/4 cup = 4 tbsp = 12 tsp = 60 ml

1 tbsp = 15 ml

Afterword

The quantities mentioned in each recipe are meant for 4 people. When I don't specify, it means you can calculate according to your taste.

I encourage anyone to experiment using their own ideas and personal taste. Only when you make fresh *pasta*, desserts, puff pastry or *pâte brisée*, you have to respect the quantities indicated.

I also advise to purchase a kitchen scale and use grams and milliliters so conversion measurements are not necessary each time, even if I have included a conversion chart at the end of the book.

When I mention aromatic herbs, these are dry herbs that I love in my cooking: garlic, rosemary, sage and chili. Readers can use fresh herbs or make dry flakes out of them. Because I use such herbs, I use much less salt which is not very good for our health.

Evo means extra virgin olive oil, which is the only oil I use in my cooking.

Thank you for the time spent reading me and forgive any mistake I might have done in English, which is not my mother tongue.

Would you have any question, please write to me and I will be very happy to help.

Happy and healthy cooking, and I hope you will love cooking *Italiano*!

Anna

A Taste of Italy

I: *Stories: With Recipes of Italian Cooking*

II: *The Extraordinary Journey of an Ordinary Woman*

III: *Cruscotto's Adventures I*

IV: *A Family Story 1924-1946*

V: *Cruscotto's Adventures II: Luna's Arrival*

VI: *Cruscotto's Adventures III: …Here Comes JoJo*

VII: *Portraits. 1861-1963*

Specials

I: *Around and About Lake Garda*

II: *Food & Wine: Recipes for a Happy Life*

III: *Italiano for Travelers*

IV: *Montichiari*

V: *If Only the Fireplace Could Speak…*

VI: *Flour: Stories & Recipes*

VII: *Travel Impressions*

VIII: *Villa San Pietro: The True Story*

Fragments of Life

I: *Perfect Imperfection*

II: *I Just Need a Pair of Pink Shoes*

III: *Keep It Simple: Thoughts on Life*

IV: *Pink Is a Life Statement*

Made in United States
Orlando, FL
23 January 2022

13945355R00040